IF THE JOB WERE EASY, I WOULDN'T NEED YOU!

IF THE JOB WERE EASY, I WOULDN'T NEED YOU!

KENNETH R. DILKS

If the Job Were Easy, I Wouldn't Need You!

ISBN 1-882185-30-7

You may contact the author by writing to:
    Kenneth R. Dilks
    c/o Cornerstone Publishing
    P.O. Box 2896
    Virginia Beach, VA 23450

Cover design and illustrations by C. Tad Crisp.

Printed in the United States of America.

To my wonderful wife, Irene, and daughter, Sonja, for their patience, understanding, love, and support.

To my daughter-in-law, Donna, who proofread my rough drafts and made several editorial improvements.

To Susan Klinefelter, who encouraged me to write the book and made me feel that there would be others who would be interested in reading it.

TABLE OF
CONTENTS

PREFACE

After several years of trying to run a company, I began to realize I had reduced the relationship with my employees to a set of sayings, albeit quaint, each having its own meaning. These sayings have become so much a part of my image and so well known by my employees that many times, all I have to do is to look at them and they say, "I know" and repeat the saying without me saying a single word.

During the first few months of 1989 while flying from one airport to another airport, I decided to write these sayings. When I got back to the office, I put a pack of 3" x 5" index cards into my briefcase and as I remembered a saying, I would write it down on a card. By late spring, I had completed the set of sayings.

In the process of writing these sayings, I decided not to include those which were obviously in the public domain, even though I may fully subscribe to the saying. I wanted these to be uniquely mine. The sayings I selected are part of my image and some have been a part of my image for so long that I have long since forgotten how I arrived at them.

I then decided to group them in some logical order. I remember a minister once saying one Sunday morning that every sermon should have three and only three points—so I decided I would group these sayings under three points. I found it was relatively easy to group the sayings by whether they related to ourselves, to others or to organizations. Once grouped, the sayings were ordered within the group. Being a frequent flyer on airlines, I found this an interesting pastime, and it gave me the chance to regroup and reorder the sayings on each flight until I finally arrived at the groupings and order in this book.

I would like to thank those many passengers who had the misfortune to sit next to me on the many airline flights and patiently listen to my explanations of each saying.

I would also like to thank my employees who gracefully put up with the sayings over the years. Their patience and tolerance has led me to believe there may be some value to the sayings (but let's face it; I was their boss). I sincerely hope, however, that your time spent reading this book will be both enjoyable and informative.

INTRODUCTION

After many years in the business world, I have found that almost all problems encountered by employees are not due to the actual work the employee is performing but due to the manner in which the employee relates to himself, relates to others, or relates to the organization. This remains true when he leaves the work environment and enters into social and private life.

As a manager, it is my job to maximize the productivity of each employee under my supervision. The obvious method to increase an employee's productivity is to allow the employee to gain experience. Any manager can accomplish this simply by giving the employee time to gain the experience.

I found that time in and of itself does not always lead to greater productivity. As I tried to analyze the many and various reasons why an employee's productivity did not increase or did not increase rapidly enough, I discovered other factors even more important than time. Even though I did not realize it at the time, these factors were the inability of an employee to relate effectively to himself, to others, and to organizations.

With each employee, I would attempt to try to understand what was hindering his growth. I found in my attempt to help him, I would use examples found in my own life or in the lives of people about whom I either knew directly or indirectly to help explain the point I was trying to make. Many of these examples could be summarized as a single saying. In many cases, this single saying would be identical to a saying I had given to another employee in a previous setting.

It was only after my first experience of having an employee so carefully explain a particular problem to me, and with me merely looking at him with that look I have in these circumstances, and having the employee respond by saying, "I know" and citing one of my sayings verbatim as I would have said it, that I realized I had reduced my relationships with my employees to a collection of sayings.

Upon reflection, I feel all problems are grouped into the same three categories. I have yet to determine which group is most important. I am not sure if it is even worth determining which group is most important.

The first group, Relating to Ourselves, was designed to help you accept your own position within our vast society. I have found very few people who realistically know their place. They either place themselves below or above their appropriate place—mostly below their appropriate place. Of even greater importance, they are unable to accept that societies range in ability according to the normal distribution curve. They seem to think almost everyone is similar to themselves. Unless you are in the center of the normal distribution curve where there are more people like you, you will find you are simply different from others—in almost all aspects, abilities, interests, and temperament.

The second group, Relating to Others, was designed to help you to relate to the many others in your day-to-day life. I have found that most people take far too seriously the acts of others, especially in close relationships such as in marriages, family, and work. They seem to place an importance to their immediate emotions and beliefs that are not justified when taken into consideration in the wider picture of the many emotions and beliefs of others.

The third group, Relating to Organizations, was designed to help you accept the role of an organization, the goals of an organization, the strength of an organization, and the weakness of an organization. Many people attribute to organizations characteristics which are simply not there. What they are classifying as characteristics are in reality their personal reaction to a stance taken by an organization. How else can you explain the many different versions you hear about the characteristics of an organization?

I hope you will find these sayings helpful in living your life. Life is just too precious and enjoyable—no matter what your position in the world's order—not to live to the fullest with no artificial restrictions placed on it by yourself.

Chapter 1

RELATING
TO
OURSELVES

50% of all people are below average
according to whatever criterion you choose.

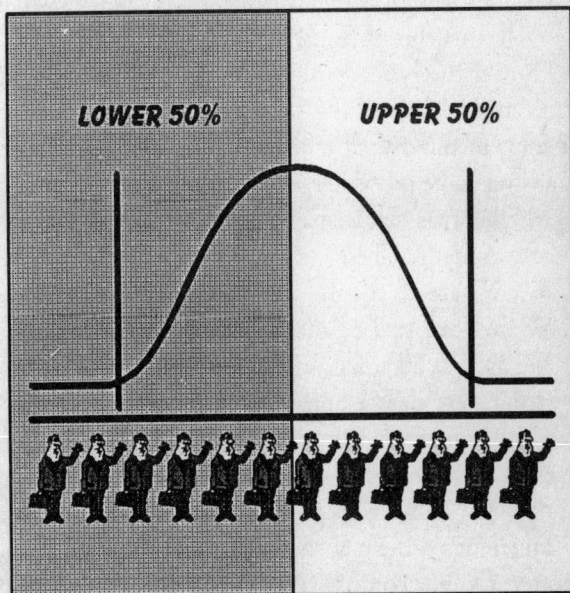

50% OF ALL PEOPLE ARE BELOW AVERAGE
ACCORDING TO WHATEVER CRITERION YOU CHOOSE.

LOWER 50%   UPPER 50%

This is one of the most difficult concepts for my employees to understand. Maybe this is the reason it's the first saying in this book. It's the basis for many of the sayings to follow.

It is my belief that a group's ability is distributed according to the normal distribution curve—commonly called a bell curve. As you analyze the normal distribution curve, you will observe that half of the people are above the midpoint and half of the people are below the midpoint *by design*. Also, the majority of the people lie around the center of the curve stating that the majority of the people are average. As you go in either direction, the number of people possessing the corresponding capability decreases until there is only one person who is the very best and only one person who is the very worst.

Well, isn't this obvious? The answer is both yes and no. From a purely academic point of view, the answer is definitely yes. But trying to use this concept to place ourselves in the overall scheme of things, I have found the answer to be no. Why?

My theory is that we have become confused as the result of two myths. These are:

- We are all equal.
- We must all be successful.

We are *not* all equal. The normal distribution curve shows that very clearly. Some of us are simply better than others according to whatever criterion you choose. There seems to be nothing we can do about it. In everything you do—your job, your community, and even your family and friends—there always seems to be someone who is better. Do not confuse being created equal with having equal opportunity!

In addition, we are taught we must be successful. Our heroes are the Horatio Alger, Robert Redford and Joe Montana. Unless we achieve these levels of success, we consider ourselves failures.

How do we resolve this dilemma? The answer is simple, and it lies in the words "according to whatever criterion you choose." Simply put, pick your own criterion. If you find yourself in a position where your relative place is not where you want to be according to your current criterion, change your criterion.

If you are a lawyer in the bottom half of the lawyers in your current community, then choose a community where you would be in the top half of the lawyers. This increases your chance of winning a case by ensuring the lawyer pitted against you is not as good as you are. It's the "big fish in the little pond" syndrome.

My advice to my employees and also my friends and family is to pick the criterion carefully to maximize your chance of success. You can't change not being equal and you have little chance of changing the pressure of trying to be successful, so therefore choose the environment in which you can be successful. A secondary reason for this saying is to teach people to accept others. You will continuously meet people who are in the bottom half. In fact, half of the people are in the bottom half. You can't do anything about it. They can't do anything about it. So accept it. But don't, with righteous indignation, degrade them by calling them stupid when their major crime is just not being as smart as you. Let us not forget that by using a different criterion, they may be in the top half and you may be in the bottom half.

75% of the people, however, think they are in the top 50%.

There seems to be such a negative connotation being in the bottom half that at least 75% of the people think they are in the top 50%. To prove my point, just ask anyone if they are in the top half or bottom half according to any criterion they may choose and they will probably tell you they are in the top half.

There are two reasons for this perception. The first is the negative connotation of being in the bottom half that causes people to stretch, if required, their position to the top half. The second reason—which is probably the primary reason—is that most people are clustered around the midpoint, and the real difference between someone at the 40% point and the 60% point isn't that great.

80% of the people are between the top 10% and the bottom 10%.

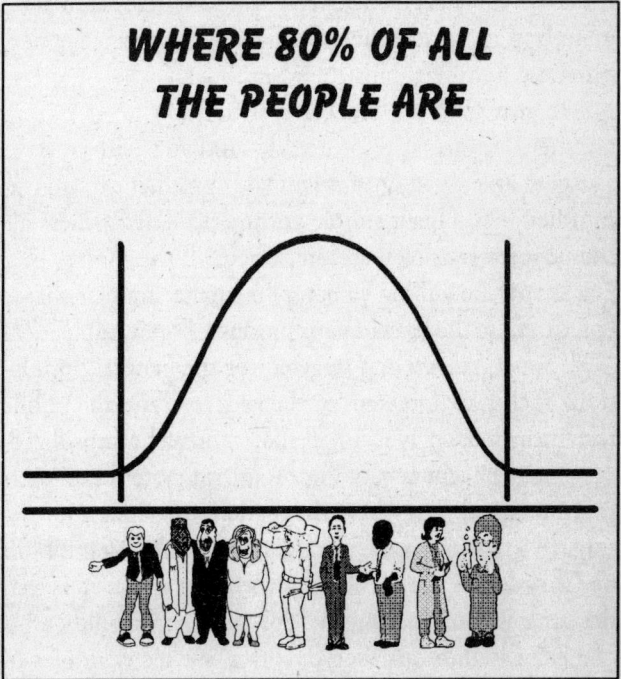

WHERE 80% OF ALL THE PEOPLE ARE

This saying is understood very well by some and not at all by others. Television networks understand it too well. They produce their programs for an audience at the ninth grade level. Newspapers also understand it. Newspapers in general also write their articles for a reader at the ninth grade level. Even the U.S. Government understands it when they require that the maintenance procedures for a system they wish to procure must be oriented to a level 5 airmen, which is at the tenth grade level.

No matter what it is, the bottom 10% will not catch on to it. They are unable to understand the television program, read the newspaper, and use the product. The top 10% finds it too easy. They find the television program boring, correct the grammar in the newspaper, and purchase a more sophisticated product.

If you wish to market a product—be it entertainment, informative or useful—and you wish to have a large market, you must orient your product toward the middle 80%. This is simple arithmetic. That's where all the people are and, therefore, where all the money is.

If you are willing to accept a smaller market share, you can raise the level of your product. For example, *The Wall Street Journal* isn't targeted for the general population. Yachts are targeted for the very few, and the public television market is so small that it must be subsidized.

This concept is very important for system designers to understand. They have the tendency to design for the top 10% to 20%. Take, for example, the M-1 tank built by Chrysler for the U.S. Army. Its major criticism is that the tank is too sophisticated for the average soldier.

Even within our everyday lives, we see examples of this. Can we perform maintenance on our cars with the electronic fuel injection system and computer controlled leveling system? How many of us can use all of the features of our new digital televisions and VCRs? Even the thermostat in my new home is programmable—that's assuming you know how to program it. System designers are developing increasingly more complex systems. The goal is to keep the human interface with the system oriented to the middle 80%, even if they are unable to keep the internal workings of the system that simple.

If you are in the top 10% of your field, expect that 90% in your field will not produce work as good as you can.

IF YOU ARE IN THE TOP 10% OF YOUR FIELD, EXPECT THAT 90% IN YOUR FIELD WILL NOT PRODUCE WORK AS GOOD AS YOU CAN.

Whenever someone is promoted from within a group to become the group's supervisor, there seems to be a problem during the first six months to a year. This stems from the new supervisor's inability to let go of the work and to let other employees perform the work. This

7

results from the fact that other workers are not able to perform the work as well as the supervisor did. From the viewpoint of higher management, this is immediately obvious. If one of his previous fellow workers could perform the work better, then that person would have been promoted to the position of supervisor.

Simply put, if you are in the top 10%, expect that 90% of your fellow workers will not produce work as good as you can. But as a supervisor, producing work is no longer your job. Getting others to produce quality work is now your job.

Higher management encounters this situation frequently. In fact, some supervisors never seem to accept the fact that others can not perform to the supervisor's level of excellence. I have found, however, that I have been successful in resolving such a situation most of the time by explaining that it is normal for subordinates not to perform as well as the supervisor and that the supervisor's job is to help the subordinates raise their level of excellence.

The bottom 10%
are in the bottom 10%.

Possibly the greatest difference between liberals and conservatives is accepting the fact that the bottom 10% are in the bottom 10%. It is at this bottom 10% where the point of diminishing returns really begins to show. It is difficult to say you should just write off the bottom 10%, but in marketing a generic product, there is no other choice.

Let us look at the normal distribution curve again. Look where the bottom 10% is. What is their constituency? Because our class system is based on merit, the upper 90% can outsmart the bottom 10% everyday.

Yes, from a political point, we cannot write off the bottom 10%. But from a marketing point, we cannot afford not to write off the bottom 10%.

From a technical point, it seems the same rule applies to system designers. We just cannot design a system to process automatically more than 90% of whatever we are processing manually. There is always that which must be manually processed.

There is one who is the worst.

THERE IS ONE WHO IS THE WORST.

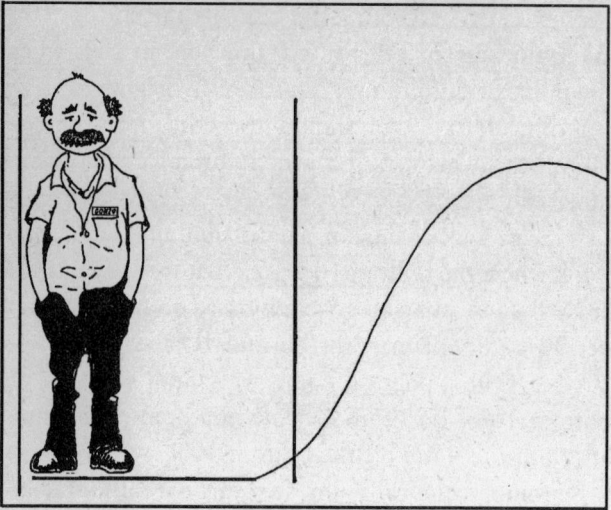

At the very far left side of the normal distribution curve is the worst one of all. There just seems to be nothing you can do about it.

There are areas in which some people claim the worst isn't that bad. For example, the worst airline pilot is supposed to have at least passed the minimum requirements to become an airline pilot. The worst medical doctor is supposed to have at least passed the minimum requirements and examinations to become a medical doctor. Let's hope so. But I just do not have enough faith in the system to believe the required examinations are so good that there is no chance for a bad one slip into the profession.

If you accept the fact that 1% of the population are real kooks, then you must accept the fact that there are 2,600,000 kooks in the U.S.

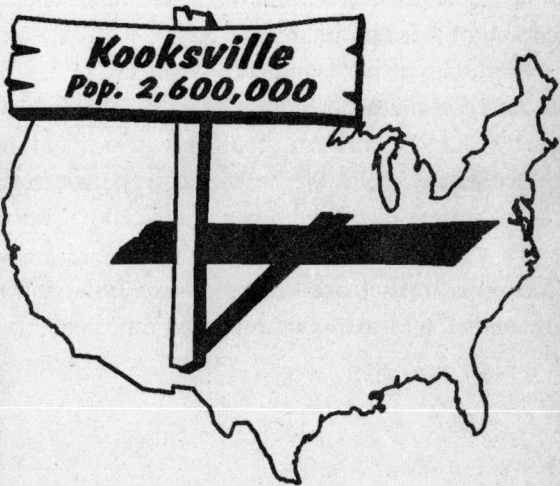

IF YOU ACCEPT THE FACT THAT 1% OF THE POPULATION ARE REAL KOOKS, THEN YOU MUST ACCEPT THE FACT THAT THERE ARE 2,600,000 KOOKS IN THE U.S.

Kooksville
Pop. 2,600,000

I have found that most people are essentially good and decent people. I have also found that even among the bottom 10%, there are still good and decent people. But there is the 1% of the population that are real kooks—and given a half a chance, they will act like real kooks.

But 2,600,000 kooks in the good old U.S. of A? No wonder we read what we read in the newspaper. No wonder newspapers such as the *National Enquirer* exist.

After my company was purchased by a large Fortune 500 corporation, I sent my personnel director to a corporate wide meeting of personnel directors. After three days, she became amazed at all the problems the other sister organizations within the corporation were encountering. Among them were lawsuits, drug usage, insubordination, and theft. My company had never encountered any of these problems.

We discussed her experience when she returned. I told her what she had discovered was due to their size. They had the 1% problem. In other words, 1% of their employees were kooks. We weren't large enough to have even a whole employee who was a kook. But I warned her that when we grew to over 100 employees, we also would begin to have our share of kooks. It's just in the mathematics, and there's nothing you can do about it.

Your ability to influence the world is like a pebble being dropped into the ocean. Your only significant influence is in the immediate vicinity of where the pebble is dropped, and it dissipates rapidly as it moves away.

How many of us during our youth thought we could change the world? We looked at the laws both natural and man-made and actually believed we could get those we felt were unfair or unjust rewritten or deleted. How utterly naive we were.

In some ways, it is good that we feel this way when we are young. Without this feeling we would not even attempt to improve the world. And even though our efforts produce very little, the results of that effort combined with the minuscule efforts of all the other young people may nudge our society toward a better place in which to live.

My primary purpose in developing this saying, however, is not to minimize the results of our effort to improve the world or rationalize our small efforts to make anyone feel better when he discovers the world is not changing very much as a result of his actions. Rather, my intention is to help everyone to live with the current laws, whether or not they are fair or just.

Productivity is greatly reduced when someone encounters a law or rule which he feels is either unfair, unjust, or just plain stupid and then attempts to change the law or rule. If he would simply accept the law or rule, he would finish the job much sooner. One of the signs of maturity is the recognition of what one can realistically do and not fight that proverbial "windmill." (*Don Quixote* was a nice story but not a good example.)

Regardless of the rules, productivity is increased by following the rules. For example, in the business of developing major computer systems for the U.S. Government, there are times we feel our product is ancillary procedures, not computer systems. There is not a manager who does not hear continuously about performing all those silly procedures and filling out those associated forms. There are those who fight them. There are those who ignore them—that is, until they find they must perform them. There are those who attempt to find shortcuts around them. But in the end, all must perform these procedures to complete the development successfully.

How much easier it would be if all your employees would simply follow the rules? There are times to discuss the rules. There are even ways to change the rules—but not during the development stage.

Let us all realize the limitations of our influence over the world and accept the world and its people as they are.

No matter how bad an earlier event may have seemed at the time, it doesn't seem so bad now.

People take things too seriously. They seem to live from one crisis to the next crisis. When something happens that is not exactly the way they want it to happen, they panic.

My usual response to an employee who is experiencing a "crisis" is to ask a simple question: "Within the last five years, what is the worst thing that has happened to you?" They tell me and then I say, "It doesn't seem so bad now, does it?"

Even the very bad things—such as a death in the family, a serious injury or illness, or a divorce—mellow with time. Everybody dies at one time in their life. It is rare when someone does not encounter injuries or illness. And what can I say about divorce? It is as common as apple pie.

But we survive these experiences. In some cases, we laugh about the bad experience. In others, we wear the experience as a badge. In most cases, we remember only the good aspects of the experience. But in all cases, its importance to us decreases with time as we try to live our lives today.

To get a proper perspective on what I am trying to say, just spend some time with a teenager and listen to the great and earth-shattering problems he must endure. You sit and listen and you wish your life was so simple. What is so earth-shattering about not having a date Sat-

15

urday night? Would you die over such a fate? Would your social life be completely destroyed if you didn't get that new dress?

Surely, someone older than you must be thinking the same things about you when you describe your great and earth-shattering problems to them. All you have to do is to extrapolate your current experience forward and realize how you will feel many years from now. When you look at the "big picture," your problems will not seem as bad.

We have no problems in life, only challenges.

I truly believe that during the final judgment, we will be graded on a relative scale. Your grade will be based on what you have done with what you got. Therefore, I believe that life is filled with challenges and that our way of meeting them armed with our assets will be the only thing graded.

A problem implies a crisis, albeit major or minor. Mr. Webster defines a problem to be:

> any question or matter involving doubt, uncertainty, or difficulty.

At the same time, Mr. Webster defines challenge:

> a call or summons to engage in any contest, as of skill, strength.

But that is the first definition for the word challenge. Let's look at the eighth definition:

> difficulty in a job or undertaking that is stimulating to one engaged in it.

The average person treats a problem as a crisis rather than a stimulating challenge. The key words in these definitions are (1) contest and (2) stimulating. We should treat the problem as playing a stimulating contest.

This is a way of looking at life which is, at first, very difficult to achieve. There will always be some problems that will be overwhelming to anyone except the very, very experienced. But this does not mean that all problems must be a crisis. If you consciously try to treat every problem as a contest and feel stimulated trying to play that contest, life will become a real joy.

Even saying that, I do divide problems into two categories:

> Legitimate problems — those problems
> you have little control in avoiding.

> Stupid problems — those problems you
> have caused yourself.

Examples of legitimate problems are family illness, death, and unexpected duties at the office. Stupid problems are the results of doing something you were told not to do, such as having your driving license suspended due to many speeding tickets. I do not classify stupid problems as challenges, just stupidity. Any stimulation received from solving stupid problems is the product of a sick mind.

Everything in moderation, including moderation.

I have met many people and I know you have met many people who go full out all the time. They are constantly running everywhere and sometimes they are running nowhere. They work too much, they play too much, they eat too much, they drink too much, and it catches up with them. (I have discovered years after I started using this saying that it was originally said by Ben Franklin. Therefore, I must give Ben credit even though this saying has become an integral part of my life.)

Life is too short to live it with that intensity. Going at that speed causes you to miss many things. You miss the joy of a sunrise, the joy of seeing your children grow up, and the joy of someone else's presence.

Emotionally, you cannot take the intensity of full speed ahead. Physically, your body cannot take the intensity of full speed ahead. Psychologically, your mind cannot function continuously at full speed ahead.

It is the psychological aspects of "full speed ahead" that bothers me most. A driven person has problems—many times, very serious problems—because he is driven at the sacrifice of many other good parts of life. I have through the years learned never to trust a driven person since I do not know what drives him. I cannot predict what he will do.

The flip side of one operating at a continuous full speed ahead is one who is barely moving. I think the key characteristic of this person is procrastination. This

19

person never gets anything done. There are many reasons for procrastination, yet none of them valid. You can trust a procrastinator—that is, you can trust him never to finish anything he starts!

After this dissertation on the merits of moderation, keep in mind that you don't be moderate all the time. Every once in a while, let your hair down. Work your tail off. Lay back and do nothing. Even given all the good points on moderation, forget moderation every so often. It's good for the psyche.

If you find yourself having difficulty getting around to doing something, it's probably because you don't want to do it badly enough.

I have found that in almost every time someone has difficulty in getting around to doing something, there is that lack of drive in wanting to do that something. The person just doesn't want to do it badly enough.

The reasons for not wanting to do something are various. They range from no interest whatsoever to fear of failing. There are many ways of accomplishing any task, and it seems that only a strong desire enables one to perform that task.

I remember years ago after I completed college, many of my former classmates decided to tour Europe with plans to just goof off during the summer before they would embark on their careers. I really wanted to go with them, but because I had student loans to pay, I could not go with them, or so I thought. It was only after a year of feeling sorry for myself and being very envious of these former classmates that I realized the only reason I was not in Europe was because I didn't want to be in Europe badly enough. I even decided that touring Europe was not enough. Within thirty days of job interviewing, I arrived in Germany with a job in my chosen field for what was to be the beginning of the best years of my life. All I had to do was to want it badly enough.

If you are having difficulty solving a problem, it could be the problem is difficult to solve.

I have never understood why so many people under evaluate themselves. I seem to encounter this continuously in my position as an executive. Whenever they begin to have difficulty in solving a problem, they immediately begin to think there is something wrong with them. Have they ever thought it could be that the problem is difficult to solve, especially in the high-tech world in which we live? And the higher you advance within a company, the more difficult the problems become.

When we were children, any problem that took longer than a few minutes to solve seemed difficult. When we became high school students, we began to encounter real problems that took a few days to solve. At the university level, the problems took a week or two to solve. But in the real world, we can encounter problems that take as long as several years to solve.

Let's take a problem which should take two years to solve. You have barely scratched the surface after even one month. These problems are usually very complex with many facets which must be considered and solved. Do not start doubting yourself just because you haven't solved the problem immediately. It just takes time. Besides, companies generally pay the big bucks to those who solve the big problems.

There are two types of people: absolutists and statisticians. Absolutists expect to win 100% of the time. Statisticians expect to win x% (where x<100%) of the time or expect to lose (100-x)% of the time.

Most people are absolutists. They expect things to go the normal way every time. When they go to their car, they expect it to start. When they pick up the telephone, they expect it to work. When they have a commitment from another person, they expect that person to meet that commitment. If these expectations are not met, they are shattered. Notice the reaction of someone who has just been told his credit card will not be accepted. Notice the irritation of someone who has waited an extra two hours for something to be done.

As a frequent traveler, I see this all the time when a flight has been delayed or canceled. These passengers become irate at the poor person behind the counter who had absolutely nothing to do with the delay or cancellation. (My son who is a pilot for a major airline has a saying, "If you have time to spare, travel by air.")

The statistician, however, expects things to happen normally x% of the time. For example, if he expects people to be on time 70% of the time, he also expects people to be late 30% of the time. Since he does not expect people to be on time all the time, he does not get upset when they are late. Also, he knows that over the course of one year, the distribution of on-time arrivals will not be even. There will be some periods of time when almost everyone will be on time and there will be some periods of time when almost everyone will be late.

A statistician knows there is nothing that occurs 100% of the time. Therefore, x is always less than 100%. While being a statistician is better psychologically than being an absolutist, statisticians range from optimistic statisticians (those who expectations are always in the 90th percentile) and pessimistic statisticians (those who expectations are always in the 10th percentile). Both extremes are unrealistic.

I have used this saying many times. For example, if you are turned down for a mortgage for that dream-house, simply reapply to other mortgage companies. If all the other mortgage companies turn you down, find another dream-house. Anytime you have you heart set on one and only one thing, you will be disappointed—maybe not this time, but you will eventually be disappointed. Realize there are more fish in the sea and simply start searching for another fish.

Life operates by the 80/20 rule: 20% of the effort produces the first 80% of the work, while 80% of the effort produces the final 20% of the work

This rule haunts me everyday of my life. People are continuously underestimating the effort to complete a task. The primary reason for this is that they do not plan enough, design enough, and just think about it enough before they start the work. This means that much of the 80% effort that produces only 20% of the work is re-work of subtasks previously thought to be complete.

Another reason for this rule is that people normally perform the easy subtasks first, especially those that have a highly visible output. This gives the impression of accomplishing a lot. It really looks good to the boss, and it can justify a 40-hour work week.

When it reaches the last 20% of the work, everything changes. You work and work and work and you just don't seem to get the job done. Your boss begins getting nervous and is breathing down your neck. And whatever happened to that 40-hour work week? You know you are in this phase when your child asks your wife, "Who is that strange man?"

My biggest problem has been computing the profit on a firm fixed price contract. Profit during the midterm of a contract is computed on a percentage-of-completion basis. In other words, if you are 50% complete and you have spent 50% of the costs, then you can

book 50% of the estimated profit. This method works fine until you reach the 80% completion point. You have spent 80% of the projected costs, you have booked 80% of the estimated profit, and you are estimating that the cost to complete as being right on target.

Then something happens. You suddenly find it will take twice as much effort to finish a subtask. Then the next subtask begins to take longer than planned. And suddenly your cost to complete increases. Your cost to date is not longer 80%, but 75% of the total estimated cost to complete. But wait a minute, you have already booked 80% of the estimated profit, a profit figure that doesn't exist anymore. And you have to make an adjustment. The only way to make that adjustment is to book a loss, sometimes significant, for the month the adjustment is made—even though you may still make a profit for the contract, all because of the 80/20 rule.

Chapter 2

RELATING
TO
OTHERS

Love is when you consciously do
something nice for your loved
one when you really want to do
something completely selfish.

We have been sold a bill of goods with the prevailing concept of love in our society. It is sold as something natural, something you do when you meet the right one, something that overcomes all obstacles. It is epitomized with clichés such as "Love is when you never have to say you're sorry."

Love is not natural. Natural is continuously looking after yourself. Natural is survival. Natural is doing that which makes you feel good. Granted, there is a special relationship between a mother and her child. This is needed to protect the child until the child is able to protect himself. But again, this is survival, not necessarily individual survival but the survival of humans as a species. This special relationship develops from the child for a significant period of time, and then becomes an extension of the mother. We call this special relationship "mother's love." This is a different type of love than the type of love between two adults.

When I first was married, this popular concept of love bothered me a great deal. I felt that I loved my wife, but it wasn't like the kind of love I saw in the movies, sung in the many love songs I heard, or written in the many books around at that time that I read.

It took me approximately two years to realize either (1) the popular concept of love didn't exist or (2) my type of love was different. I finally came to the conclusion that the popular concept of love didn't exist. But was what I was experiencing really love? The answer was yes. In the same manner that you cannot love a perfect person, you cannot love if you are a perfect person. My wife and I have to try to understand each other, to forgive each other many, many times, and to compromise with each other if we were ever to do things together.

If love is forgiveness, then the other person had to have done something to be forgiven. Surely, if you had to be forgiven, shouldn't you say "I'm sorry"? And why did you do something for which you needed to be forgiven and for which to be sorry? Simple, you were thinking of yourself. You wanted to do something for yourself. You were thinking of your feelings only. You probably didn't mean to hurt your loved one. You were just being selfish.

Love is realizing that these are your feelings and consciously deciding to do something nice for your loved one when you really want to do that something completely selfish. The conscious decision to do something nice is love. If to do something nice for someone else was natural, it wouldn't be love; it would just be natural. Don't feel guilty about doing these acts consciously.

When your acts of doing something nice for your loved one start to become natural, begin to worry. You are beginning to lose it. Begin to think of what your loved one really would like to do or really would like to hear. Make it conscious again.

Marital arithmetic proves that 80+80=100. In other words, if you feel you are giving in 80% of the time and your spouse feels they are giving in 80% of the time, then it is approximately even.

Several years ago when my oldest son was sixteen, he and his girlfriend were sitting at the supper table with the rest of our family when they began an argument. The argument centered on the fact that both felt they were giving in to the other all the time. Both would say that they were always doing what the other wanted to do. My wife and I listened to the argument for several minutes before we realized they were both giving in to the other about the same number of times. But they both felt they were giving in approximately 80% of the time.

It was then I began to realize that if your relationship with your loved one is to be approximately even or balanced, it must seem to be weighed heavily on your side. When you think about it, it is obvious. You live continuously in your own mind. You are constantly aware of what your mind is thinking, planning, and wanting. You are not aware of what is going on in your loved-one's mind. When you knew you really wanted to do something else, you probably didn't communicate that to your loved one. You gave, therefore, the impression you wanted to do what your loved one wanted to do. And that is where the difference lies.

The lesson I learned from that one evening and the many hours I have thought about that evening is to make sure I feel I have given in approximately 80% of the time before I feel the relationship is all me giving and giving. I know I don't always communicate what I really want to do all the time and I feel shouldn't. I do know that more times than not when I do communicate what I really want to do, we usually do what I want to do when she does not say anything. When she does say something, that's different. Then we discuss the matter until we do either what I want to do, what she wants to do or what neither one of us originally wanted to do.

But when she does not say anything, it does not mean we will do something she wants to do. It only means she did not say anything. If all of our thoughts were communicated to each other, it would be obvious as to the number of times one gives in to the other. But we don't always communicate our desires and I don't think we should because we would then be constantly bickering over what we would be doing. We just accept that there are these uncommunicated desires on the other person's part.

If you are a husband and you feel hard done by your wife, just talk to another husband.

I realized when I use the expression "hard done by," many Americans may not understand what I mean by it. Having married an English girl, I have adopted many of their expressions. By saying one is "hard done by" by another, they mean they are having a rough time with the relationship and they are on the short end of it all.

I don't think I have ever met another husband who hasn't complained about how illogical some of his wife's actions are. You listen to him talk for a while and you swear he is talking about your own wife and you wonder how he got to know your wife so well.

I know that most men have come to the conclusion that all women are made from the same mold. They find they have a great deal of difficulty understanding them, if at all. They have virtually no ability to predict their actions except that their actions will be unpredictable. Logic seems completely alien to them.

I feel it is especially difficult for those of us who are formally trained in the sciences. The scientific method was our life and it has become our mistress. We are forced to be logical during our entire business day. Then we go home. We find that what works at the office does not work at home. We knew it didn't work with the children, but then they were children. But my wife! She is an adult. She should understand logic. Doesn't everyone understand logic?

34

Talking to another husband helps if you find yourself in this situation. You find he has exactly the same problems with his wife you have with your wife. These conversations are probably what saves many marriages. You quickly realize the grass is not greener on the other side of the fence. You quickly realize that women are all made from the same mold and that if you leave the woman you have, you will find the next woman will be approximately the same, especially in your ability to understand her.

If you are a wife and you feel hard done by your husband, just talk to another wife.

Then I talked to my wife and her conversation about men sounded, in her own way, very similar to what we men say about women. I have come to the conclusion that men and women are different. We will never even begin to understand each other. And the only solution to this dilemma is to love each other, accept and not try to change each other, forgive each other, and consciously try to do something nice for each other when what you really want to do is something completely selfish.

Go to your room.

The saying, "Go to your room," is more indicative of my relationship with my employees than it is a saying of great philosophical meaning. I use this saying in response to an employee's statement that is obviously lacking in common sense. In the vast majority of the times, the employee realizes this before he even finishes what he is saying. "Go to your room" is more a saying a father would say to his children. In the context I use it, it is said more in jest than in seriousness. It generally elicits a smile or laughter, especially when they say "I know, go to my room" before I have a chance to say it.

I guess it is my belief that an executive should act as the benevolent philosopher king—in much the same manner as a father should act in his home over his dominions—that really started me using this saying. These employees are family and your job is to protect them in a similar manner as your own family. They are not just an entry in a Lotus 1-2-3 spread sheet but real honest-to-goodness people with feelings and desires of their own. I have found that the vast majority of people are good people with varying degrees of talent but almost always a great desire to do a good job. Their major problem, many times, is their inability to know how to do that good job.

That's the job of the executive among mahogany row or a frontline supervisor. Teach and guide employees so that they can accomplish their goals. Don't misinterpret an employee's inability to know how to accomplish their goals as the employee's deficiency. It is your deficiency, at least up to the point of diminishing returns. (I will accept that there are some employees which require so much guidance, the company cannot afford the learning process.)

I do not think my saying, "Go to your room," has ever been misinterpreted by any of my employees. They understand the context in which it is said. They accepted the fact that the saying was in response to something they said which was really silly.

Each extended family has the following positions: Patriarch, Matriarch, Saint, Black Sheep

Through the many years of my life, I have discovered that every extended family has certain distinct positions. First, let me define the term "extended family" to mean your immediate family (your spouse, your children), both sets of parents, aunt and uncles, and their children with whom you have some kind of relationship, even if it was when you were very young.

In many cases, an extended family may have a void of a position due to a death in the family, but in almost every case, this void will be filled within a very short time.

The most important of these positions are the patriarch and the matriarch. These two are the ones the entire family defers in regard to matters of the family. They ask guidance of them. They adopt the standards from them. They feel the presence of them whenever they are doing something they feel would not be approved, even though the patriarch or matriarch is not there.

The patriarch and matriarch are rarely married to each other. I am not sure they could really stand each other. Both have a power of personality which would seem overbearing to the other. They are not always of the same generation. While mostly they are of the older generation, I have seem cases where one of a younger generation reaches this status, primarily due to the success of that person. For example, if a man was the first to obtain a college education and has used that education effectively to become a success in his career, by virtue of being the first and sometimes the only one with that status, the extended family defers the title of patriarch to him.

Then there is the family saint. Everybody knows who he is. He is the one with the sweetest personality. He is the one upon whom everyone can always depend.

In my family, the saint was an uncle who was born with a disease that caused him not to have full dexterity. He never married. He was an orderly in the local hospital. But his feats became famous. No matter what needed to be done, he would do it. There was no such thing as a 40-hour week for this man. He was constantly helping other people with a smile and words that just made you feel great.

He even became a mediator between the warring factions of his family, never understanding why they acted the way they did, only understanding that he loved both sides. Both sides knew he was helping the other side but he was so easily loved, they never felt he was against one side by helping the other.

Then there is the proverbial black sheep. This is the member of the extended family about whom the other members only whisper. You know who I mean. He is your Uncle Charlie, the drunkard. He is cousin Bill, who has served time in jail. I have seen some people who boasted of being the black sheep, but when you begin to investigate their claim, they were just rebellious during their youth. There really was another person in their extended family who really qualified as the black sheep.

If your children are grown, they will discuss matters of the heart with the mother and matters of the pocketbook with the father.

I am still angry at my mother for not briefing me on what I would experience as a parent. The point is, she knew. She knew from direct experience. Still, she didn't tell me what to expect. She claims I would not have listened. She is probably right. In fact, there are times when I think that if all of us had been briefed on the trials and tribulations of being a parent, and if we had listened, we would not have had any children.

Still, the one thing that surprised me the most was the relationship I would have with the children when they became adults. Even by late puberty, they had divided their world into three parts. The part they discussed with their mothers, the part they discussed with their fathers, and the part they never discussed with their parents—at least at the time the subject was germane.

It is only because my wife and I discussed things together that I even knew that my children discussed different things with her. And it always seemed to be matters of the heart. "Should I date that boy? What should I buy for my girlfriend for her birthday? Mom, we had an argument last night; what should I do about it?" With me, it was always the same subject: "Dad, can I borrow $5?" Oh, that was when they were young. Now it is: "Can I borrow $5,000 to make that down payment on this beautiful house?"

The generations are different today then they were when I was growing up. Then, a major milestone was: Will I make enough money to take my parents out to dinner? The really major milestone was when they came to your house for Thanksgiving dinner. These were signs of achieving real adult status with your parents—at least to some degree.

But to the kids of my children's generation, the depression is only a period about which they read during history class. My lifetime is already in the history books. We were proud of rising up from the depression years. My kids knew only the affluence of our adult lives.

The ultimate, though, is when your children come to your house—I emphasize "your house"—and tell their mother they are separating from their spouse. Then they tell you they want to move back with the grandchildren. It will only be for a little while, they say. A year later you begin to realize relative adjectives have different meanings to their generation than they do to your generation. You thought the expression, "a little while," meant one or two months—not one or two years!

Just once, I would like for the roles between my wife and I to be reversed. I feel I have some experience in matters of the heart and certainly my wife has some experience in matters of the pocketbook. Just once I would like them to talk to me about their love lives and let my wife handle the financial matters. Maybe not, the generation differences are great enough for me not to understand their needs in the manner they wish. At least in the financial arena, we have the hard, cold world of mathematics guiding us. Who can argue that it takes so much money a month to pay off that loan they want?

People will normally become exactly what you expect of them.

The vast majority of people in this world—at least the vast majority of the people in the top 90%—will normally become exactly what you expect of them. If you truly expect them to be successful and you treat them as if you truly expect them to be successful, they will become successful. If you truly expect them to be failures and you treat them as if you truly expect them to be failures, they will become failures. And I'm talking about the same people. An old adage in the business world is that if you are having trouble with an organization, just replace the top guy. In other words, its not the people, its what is expected of the people.

I grew up in North Carolina where they had a most unusual school bus system. Their system was one of the largest in the United States in both the number of school buses and the number of miles driven. Yet with the exception of one county, the only way you could get a school bus driving license was to (1) have a regular driving license, (2) pass the school bus driving license test and (3) be a full time student at the local high school. You would lose your school bus driving license by (1) having any moving violation, regardless of whether it was in the school bus or in your private car and (2) graduating from high school.

I would meet people from other states who were horrified at the prospects their children would be driven to school by children. Yet North Carolina had the best safety record of any school bus system in the United

States. Why? They expected these high school kids to be professional—and because they were expected to be professionals, they became professionals. And their safety record showed they were professionals.

I have found this lesson to be most helpful in managing people. I have consistently found that people who felt they were not qualified to perform a task—by both expecting them to perform and treating them as if I expected them to perform— performed the task. This has happened so often I am convinced this saying is one of the truisms of life.

You must temper this with realism, however. You cannot expect someone to perform at levels at which he just cannot. But my experience is that most people can operate at a level significantly above what they normally think they can operate. It takes some practice at choosing the right level, but it can be done.

There is another aspect of this saying that is much more insidious—whether you expect everyone to be trustworthy or not. I have found that the same person will generally be trustworthy to those who trust them and will not be trustworthy to those who distrust everyone. There is a mental health problem for those who distrust everyone constantly; they live with a fear that everyone is out to get them. For those trusting people, however, the many years of fearless living far outweighs those few moments when those very few violate your trust.

Never fight a battle unless you have a high probability of winning.

This has been the most difficult saying for me to follow. With many of my family and friends, it has been even more difficult. If they feel they are right, they want to go out and fight the battle. I am not talking about battles with windmills. I am talking about cases where you really feel you are right and you have been unjustly harmed, albeit maybe just your ego.

It is important to me that you understand me clearly here. I am not saying you should sit back and take everything dished out to you, especially when you have been harmed. What I am saying is there are enough battles to fight without fighting those you have a low probability of winning.

Let me give you a few examples. Remember, many of my experiences have been in the development of state-of-the-art computer systems for the U.S. Government, meaning that I must live with the government regulations. Invariably, an employee will see some regulation that he feels is simply stupid. This regulation hinders him from doing his job efficiently; it takes him away from the work he loves, because he just does not understand the purpose of the regulation.

This is where I counsel him to meet the regulation. He will not change the regulation, especially within the time frame of the project. Any time spent in trying to change the regulation will be time wasted. And besides, there is the blow to the person's ego when he finally realizes he has failed in fighting this battle. We don't like failures. It tends to destroy our confidence.

To put this saying in even more perspective, think of some of the battles you have fought in the past where it was obvious from the beginning you had a low probability of winning and you eventually lost the battle. Does it seem so important today? Couldn't you have spent your time doing better things? Wasn't there some other battle with a higher probability of winning you could have fought?

My brother-in-law recently spent a lot of time complaining about all the documents he had to sign at the closing of the purchase of his house. And yes, from his viewpoint, many of these documents seemed ridiculous. But in the final analysis, he and his wife had to sign each and every one of those documents. It was time spent doomed to futility. There was no way he could have changed any step of the process during the closing ceremony. So why fight it?

Even if you have a high probability of winning a battle, don't fight the battle unless you have something to gain from winning the battle.

If you think the previous saying is difficult to follow, try this one. Even if you can win the battle, are you going to gain anything from it? The reasoning behind these sayings is that we only have so much time in our lives and we must spend this time wisely. But we tend to fight battles where the only gain is the satisfaction that we have won the battle. If there were no other battles to fight, then maybe, just maybe, the satisfaction of winning with no gain would be enough. But I have never had that luxury of not having other battles to fight.

The determination of whether to fight a battle is directly related to the amount of gain. For example, to fight a battle against all odds when to lose would mean the loss of your driving license may be worth it. I did that once when the Commonwealth of Virginia was threatening to take away my son's driving license. At his age of 18 and still in high school, my wife and I knew that the only people who would be punished would be us since we would have to drive him here and there, mostly at inopportune times. I fought and eventually I won this battle. But, on the other hand, if I got caught speeding and it was obvious I was speeding, I might as well pay my speeding ticket and go on with my life.

Now if you have a high probability of winning and you have something to gain by winning, fight that battle.

Most people do not think enough of you to say bad things about you intentionally. They are only thinking of themselves when they are saying the bad things.

I guess this saying is my form of "I'm okay; you're okay." I am simply saying to my employees—and my family and close friends—don't take what has just been said to you seriously. It is normally their problem, not your problem.

I only have to look at my own experiences to prove this point. Let's say I'm having a bad day. Everything is going wrong. During my drive home, this idiot pulls in front of me and almost causes an accident. I walk into my house and when my wife says something very trivial, I jump down her throat, even though she didn't even do anything wrong! The problem is me.

This occurs in a relationship in which I care for her. Now, take a relationship where there is no caring. Let's say you are at a store trying to buy something. You don't know this person from Adam. And they are having a bad day and they jump down your throat for something extremely trivial. Don't get upset. It's not you; it's them. Don't let your stomach get twisted up over something which you can not control. Don't get angry, because it is a battle you cannot win. People in this state are illogical and are extremely unreasonable. Walk away from it and enjoy those people who have not had a bad day.

I know it is very difficult not to take what other people say to you personally. I have a great deal of difficulty with this saying myself, especially when someone accuses me falsely. I know I should consider the source, but it still hurts. I find, however, I can follow this saying more easily the further away the person is from me emotionally. With most complete strangers, I can follow this saying easily. The closer the person is to me, the more difficult it is for me. When I reach my immediate family, it becomes extremely difficult for me to accept that they are only thinking of themselves when they are saying those bad things. It is in these close relationships where the saying should be followed most closely.

Most people do not think enough of you to listen to what you have to say.

I have found that most people do not listen, but spend all their time during a conversation thinking of what they will say when they get their chance. I am also guilty of this.

It seems the more articulate a person is, the more guilty he is of not listening. Why? We spend our entire conscious life within that little head of ours. We are aware of all our thoughts. We are aware of all the inputs from our senses. We can be hearing someone speak, but also be aware of a background sound. At the same time, we can be aware of something completely different that we are seeing, touching, tasting, or smelling. We are conscious of all of these, including our internal thoughts.

The other person is not conscious of any of our inputs from our senses or our internal thoughts. Yes, they are conscious of all of their inputs from their senses and their internal thoughts, but not of ours. Therefore, what you say is normally a small percentage of the inputs to the other person's minds. And based on what is being said, the frame of mind of the listener and many other factors, the probability of the other person is really listening to you is very small.

Now, don't feel shattered by this loss of importance. Let's face it, the most important person in that person's life is himself. It's true with you. Why shouldn't it be true with them? It happens all the time in even the best of relationships.

There is, however, something you can do about it. Even if you have to play it as a game, try to make understanding someone—especially someone very close to you—important. It is very difficult. Concentrate and listen to every word. Observe the expression on their face, for the face communicates almost as much as the words do. Look at the body movement, less you miss even more communication.

People will begin to feel you have become their best friend in the world, simply by listening and observing them as if they are the most important thing in the world at that moment. Think of those you consider friends. Don't they hang on your every word? I know my friends do. Try this and you will find it very satisfying.

Everybody normally has at least one subject about which he knows more than 90% than the people he knows.

I have found that everyone has at least one subject about which he knows more than 90% than the people he knows. And if you let him talk about that subject, he is happier than a lark.

This is true no matter what station the person has in our society. Everyone has at least one subject. The secret is to identify that subject. You can change the worst introverted person into the most talkative person alive simply by discovering his favorite subject. I have even found mentally challenged adults very knowledgeable about a subject—so I am convinced my thesis is true.

Listening to someone speak about his favorite subject enables him to begin to feel a degree of importance that is necessary to build confidence in life. Your listening is good for that person—and if you listen carefully enough, you may even learn something.

Again, it is important for you to learn to listen. And this is very difficult for anyone to do, especially if you are in the top 10% to 20%. You know more than the majority of the people around you or you would not be in the top 10% to 20%. But this person knows more about at least one subject than you, even if it is nothing more than directions through a strange city. Search for that subject and listen.

53

If you want to have a conversation with someone so that he considers it an interesting one, talk about something in which he is interested.

You would be amazed how this works. First find out the subject in which the other person is really interested. Then begin to discuss that subject, and as you begin to finish the conversation, he will end it by saying something like: "I really enjoyed talking with you." or "That was really an interesting conversation." To him, it was.

Why? You discussed a subject in which he had a great deal of interest. Yes, it was interesting to him. It was his subject. Yes, he enjoyed talking with you. You talked about a subject in which he was very interested. All of this seems a little callous? No, it is not. It is simply the art of being a good conversationalist. And more importantly, it is simply the art of making the other person feel good. You are making the other person your most interesting subject.

It sounds simple, but it is extremely difficult to do. If you are normal, you will be more interested in yourself than you are in others. This is the way you were born; this is the way you were raised; and this is the way you have been all of your life. But just try it. Listen to every word the other person is saying. Get interested in both the subject and in the person who is talking. You will find a completely different feeling developing inside of you. It is a good feeling. I know. I have felt it. But sadly to say, not as often as I should.

Your part of the conversation should be restricted to questions about which he obviously knows.

A most important corollary to this saying is that your part of the conversation should be restricted to questions about which he obviously knows. This is important to keep his interest up and to continue the conversation. It is very difficult for him to keep up a conversation when he begins to feel that you are not interested. If there is no dialogue from you, the conversation dies. Therefore, you must continue to ask questions about the subject.

This may all be Machiavelian. And yes, I agree, it may be. But in the same manner as love, there must be a conscious effort. So it is with interesting conversation. Let's face it, conversation is a form of a personal relationship with another human being. You reap great rewards from following this saying and its corollary both in learning new subjects and new people and in being viewed as a nice guy.

In most negotiations, one normally feels the other person has a better position from which to negotiate than you do.

This is so true, and for so many reasons. The main reason is that you enter into the negotiations knowing your limits, but you don't know the other person's limits. You know just how far you are willing to go, but you don't know how far he is willing to go. You know your limitations as a negotiator, but you don't know his limitations. So you immediately assume that the other person is an excellent negotiator. Not necessarily so. In more times than not, the other person is just like you.

The easiest advice I can give someone is to enter into all negotiations willing to walk away. Oh how simplistic that advice is. There are many situations in which walking away is just not one of the options. Take the role of being a husband, father, or a family member. You can't just walk away. You have to negotiate. The advice to be willing to walk away is not applicable, for example, if you are trying to negotiate a time your daughter must be home after a date.

Experts in negotiation seem to agree that the best negotiations result in something good being achieved by both negotiating parties. To achieve this goal, one must realize the other has his own limitations and probably, his own phobias. You must identify them and use them to arrive at a reasonable agreement.

The art of good negotiation is achieving reasonable agreements. Anything less is not good negotiating.

During a sale, the seller normally thinks the buyer has the better position from which to negotiate.

The buyer has the better position from which to negotiate in most cases. He can always elect not to buy. This is not true in the rare cases in which the buyer must buy.

It is rare that the buyer must buy. He sometimes thinks he must buy, but rarely does he really have to buy. Take, for example, a car buyer. The car is not the only car in the world and this car dealer is the only car dealer in the world. The buyer must prepare himself psychologically to be willing to walk away from the deal.

On the other side of the coin is the seller. Granted, we are in the role of buyer more often than seller, unless we are in sales. But when we must sell something, we must realize that not all buyers believe in this saying. The extreme is epitomized in the saying: "A sucker is born every minute." Make the buyer feel that what you are selling exists no where else in the world and you are the only source available.

In other words, don't automatically assume that the buyer has the better position from which to negotiate. Also, realize there is more than one fish in the sea. If this buyer doesn't want to buy, then maybe the next buyer may want to buy. When you don't appear to be too anxious. Be a statistician, not an absolutist. This saying works both ways. By realizing what is normal, you can reap advantages from either the role of being the seller or the buyer.

Chapter 3

RELATING
TO
ORGANIZATIONS

If the job were easy, I wouldn't need you.

This is definitely the most famous of all my sayings within the company. Just about everyone within the company has heard this saying directed to them.

There are two significant aspects of this saying that are germane to one's position within a company. The first is that executives generally created positions because the job has ceased to be easy. When you first start a company, in addition to producing the company's product, you must also do all those other tasks required for the proper management of a company, such as bookkeeping, payroll, and benefit program management. When you only have two or three employees, these tasks are easy. As you grow, these tasks become increasingly difficult until finally, you have to hire someone to perform the tasks. You first hire a bookkeeper. Then you grow even more and the work becomes too complex for your bookkeeper and you have to hire a comptroller. This is repeated for every small task you initially performed when you started your company until you have a large support staff. The second aspect of this saying is that the difficulty of your job justifies your salary in some respect. Granted, the market place is the final determinate of your salary, but the market place is really the law of supply and demand. If the demand is high, then the supply of qualified people will be low due to the difficulty of the job. The salary will then be high accordingly.

My primary purpose in saying this to my employ-

ees is to enable them to accept the difficulty of their job. It is the very fact the job is difficult that the job even exists and pays the salary it does. So why complain about your job security? It is your job. You have been trained for it. You have experience doing it.

This is especially true with program managers. There are some program managers who continuously complain about the many problems they are having. From my vantage point, if we didn't have those problems with the program, I could easily manage the program myself and wouldn't need that program manager. This is even true with that excellent program manager who plans the program's activities so well that no problems ever occur. Even there, I couldn't perform all that planning for my programs and perform the monitoring of the execution of my plans such that no problems would occur.

Yet, as many times as my employees have heard me say to them "If the job were easy, I wouldn't need you," they still complain about their job, and I still have to repeat the saying to them. Fortunately, however, many times, all I have to do is to look at them, and they repeat the saying back to me, and then go to their room.

If you are an executive, all easy problems will be solved by your subordinates.

A good executive learns very early in his career that he must delegate both authority and responsibility to his subordinates. He learns that he must manage his subordinates at a macro level without getting into the details very often. For example, a program manager has successfully performed his job if the contract was completed, made the projected profit, and the customer is happy. An executive does not really get into the details of how the program manager accomplished this feat. But problems always occur. An item needed by this week might not be delivered until next week, and you have to modify your plans to accommodate this change. A key employee might get sick or quit, and as an executive, you have to make some significant personnel adjustments.

The easier the problem, the lower in the organization the problem is solved. As the problem becomes increasingly more complex, the higher it goes in the organization to find the person to solve the problem—until it gets so difficult that it finds its way to your office. You rarely get easy problems to solve. (I haven't had an easy problem in years). You find there is never a simple answer. There is seldom a single answer. You must make a judgment call, the consequences of which almost always could result in loss of profit, loss of employees, or loss of a contract.

People who are not executives view an executive's job as easy. They do not view executives as having feelings. They see executives as cold and callous people who merely run our companies as entries in our Lotus 1-2-3 spread sheets. Yes, there are those who are that way, but not all of us. We lose sleep over these difficult decisions we must make. And if the job were easy, where would we be? It comes with the turf. Expect with every promotion, the problems you must solve will become more difficult. But don't forget, you are making more money. You are enjoying more perks. It is not all negative.

There is a corollary to this saying.

Objective decision making is relegated to the lowest levels of an organization. As you rise within an organization, decision making becomes more and more subjective until you reach the highest level where all decision making is subjective.

There is no question that subjective decision making is the most difficult. Take, for example, the decision of determining the profit margin on a contract. If you decide to make it too big, you lose the contract. If you decide to make it too small, you may not have enough money to pay for those ever present unpredictables which happen in all contracts. Determining the profit margin is at best a judgment call based on the subjective readings of the customer by the executive.

Subjective decision making is the domain of an executive. As we become more and more sophisticated with software programs to help in the management of a company, the more frequently decisions will be relegated to your subordinates. This means that decisions you use to make subjectively will be made objectively by subordinates. The decisions remaining for you to make will still be subjective.

Never put off until tomorrow what you can get someone else to do today.

When I first started to manage people, I had a great deal of difficulty delegating tasks to my subordinates. I knew that I could do the task better and faster then they could. My problem was that I had more tasks to perform. In fact, I had so many tasks to perform, my supervisor in all his wisdom had given me a staff to help me perform all these tasks.

I had to learn to delegate. It took at least a year for me to learn how to do it. I found that I was working day and night just to meet the department's commitments. I found that my employees were complaining about having nothing to do. I was embarrassed when my supervisor called me into his office and told me that if I didn't begin to delegate some of the tasks to my subordinates, one of those subordinates would become my supervisor, regardless of how good a worker I was.

I finally learned how to delegate, and now, I have become quite good at it—even when I know I could do the work better and faster. I delegate today what has to be done today. It has actually become easy for me to delegate. It is not my job to do the work, but to manage others who do the work.

I used to take a great deal of pride in the work I did. Being in the computer programming field, I could see my programs work, but I was limited in the number of programs I could write. Now there is no limit. If I want 100,000 lines of code to be written, I delegate the task to that number of people who can produce 100,000 lines of code in the time period required and go on to do something else. By delegating, I expand my own ability to perform. Granted, I have to establish the environment in which the 100,000 lines of code are produced. Granted, I have to establish the procedures they must be used to produce the 100,000 lines of code. And granted, I have to manage all those ancillary functions that support a company that must produce 100,000 lines of code. But I can take credit for the production of the 100,000 lines of code. Of course, I will always give credit to all of those who produced the 100,000 lines of code.

Managing a company is similar to assuring that each executive is exerting his force on a balloon such that the balloon is perfectly round.

Managing a company is a team effort. A good executive tries to surround himself with the best he can find. But the higher you go in an organization, the stronger willed people you must have. In the immediate vicinity of the president, you will find people with the strongest wills.

Each of these executives wants to do things the right way—his way. You find very quickly when you are the president, your immediate staff is constantly trying to influence you to do it his way. Your job is to balance the forces from each executive. If you allow one executive to get his way too often, you will begin to lose the other executives. First, you begin to lose their opinions because they begin to feel you do not wish to listen to them. Then you begin to lose their effectiveness because they begin to wonder why should they put out the effort. And finally you begin to lose them, as one by one, they begin to resign.

The most difficult task for a president is to balance the force his immediate staff exerts on the company. Yes, by design, some of the immediate staff should exert more force on the company than others, but the force should be balanced.

There are those executives who promote competition among the senior executives who are immediately subordinate to them. I feel that is self-defeating, and the company will never accomplish as much as if they were operating as a team. If you allow your staff to compete among themselves, you have lost control of the balance of the force necessary to be really productive.

I'm sorry to say this saying resulted from some experiences I have had whereby members of my immediate staff were fighting amongst themselves, both over policies and procedures, and over their access to me. It began to result in problems in producing our products. I had lost control of the balance I wanted between the members of my immediate management staff. It had reached a point where I had to get rid of three of the members to resolve the problem.

Since my last experience of losing control of the balance, I have tried to monitor the activities of each of my senior management staff to ensure they are all working as a team. They are not fighting among each other and their staffs feel they are working for the same company. It is at this level where the real damage is done when you lose control. It is at this level where you must exercise control to avoid real damage.

Most employees do not feel they can perform at the level management feels they can.

I have always felt that I could perform at a level significantly higher than my current position. I have always had the feeling that all I needed was to be given a chance and I would conquer the world. What a surprise it was to me when I discovered I was in a very small minority of people who had this feeling. I discovered this when I would try to promote someone to a higher position and I would constantly get resistance.

I had never experienced such a feeling of not wanting a job that was obviously an advancement. Why were others opposed to being promoted? After several years of pondering over this matter, I'm still not sure. I have some ideas, however. Perhaps the employee lacks self confidence, or is afraid to leave the security of a job they know well. Even though I have coerced some employees into their new positions and they have done the new job well, these same employees failed to learn from the experience that there is virtually nothing they could not do given the proper circumstances.

Self confidence is missing in so many people. Why? I do not know. There is a very small number of tasks that my employees could not do. They could do that task at a level of excellence such that they could be ranked with their peers in the industry. Many of the sayings in this book are oriented toward giving each person the

confidence necessary to accomplish a task. I am convinced that most lack of self confidence is the direct result
of the individual not knowing what is normal in people.
They just do not realize that even the most successful
people have the same fears they do. The difference is
simply the successful people go ahead and do whatever
they have to do to become successful in spite of their
fears. These successful people have failed many times
along the path to success. They know that success is only
one-tenth talent and nine-tenths tenacity. If more people
realized this, they would be more successful.

Feeling secure in your current position and being
unwilling to accept a new position is very dangerous.
Times are changing, and if you do not change with the
times, you will be changing your position anyway because your current position will no longer exist. So stay
ahead of the times. If you are so fortunate to be offered
a new position, accept it. Oh, you will have to learn new
things. Yes, the job is different, but that's the fun of it
all. Stop learning and you will go backwards.

No, I still do not understand.

You can only push employees to a finite, small increase in productivity.

As a supervisor, I have found you can get your employees to improve productivity only a finite, small amount. In other words, you can only change their procedures so much. Anything more and they will panic.

Change is frightening to most people. But in reality, change means job security. Yet, it is change—or rather the fear of change—that hinders productivity increases in our society. I have seen people reject change for the simple reason they do not see any reason to do their task any differently than they have for the last twenty years. So you can increase productivity a small bit. Who cares?

We should care! This type of attitude puts your job in jeopardy. If you don't change, someone else will. And that someone else will seize the market with either a better product or a lower price—perhaps both. When this happens, they have no alternative but to lay you off. If this sort of thing didn't happen, we would still have a major wagon industry in the United States.

Let us look at this saying strictly from an executive's viewpoint. When you try to make changes in the way people perform their tasks, make each change small. As soon as they are comfortable with that small change, make another small change, and so on, until you have accomplished the change you want. Allow employees to recommend changes, provided you keep them small. If the changes become too big, you will have a rebellion on your hands. You will begin to lose some of your best employees; they just will not accept big changes.

90% of all employees will evaluate themselves below that which their supervisor will.

Several years ago I instituted a program within our merit review process whereby in addition to the supervisor filling out the merit review form, the employee was requested to fill out the form as a method of self evaluation. During the review process, the supervisor and the employee compared the two forms.

In almost every case, the supervisor rated the employee higher than the employee rated himself. This became even more so when the supervisor was an experienced supervisor. The supervisor would rate a beginning programmer against other beginning programmers and a senior programmer against other senior programmers. But the employee would rate himself—regardless of his level—against the chief computer scientist.

This was so consistent that approximately 90% of all of my employees would evaluate themselves below their supervisor's evaluation. I think this may have some positive aspects to it in that as long as the employee places such strict standards on himself, he will strive to better himself each day. I also think this may have some negative aspects to it in that the employee may never quite get that feeling of achieving that is so necessary to the building of confidence. Eventually, we stopped requiring employees to evaluate themselves because in general they did not enjoy this self evaluation process.

There was another interesting aspect of this experiment. When an employee was evaluated at a superior rating at a given level and when he was promoted (e.g., from a programmer to a senior programmer), he was evaluated only at a fully competent rating. He had difficulty understanding that to receive a superior rating at the higher level position, he had to perform better. To solve this problem, we had to advise each person whom we promoted that we expected a higher level of performance from him if he was to receive the same evaluation ratings he was receiving prior to the promotion.

A few employees will always overestimate their abilities.

Needless to say, there was that 10% who would always over estimate their abilities in their self evaluation. You would compare their evaluation form with yours and you would wonder if they were the same person. From a supervisor's standpoint, it is always easier to tell an employee they are better than they feel they are than that they are not as good as they think they are. This was the primary reason why we discontinued the program of employee self evaluation.

Productivity increases only come from the employees directly involved with the production.

No matter how many reorganizations you may implement, no matter how many new reports you may require, no matter what you do—unless you change the process and environment of the employee directly involved with production—productivity will not increase.

In other words, the employee directly involved with production is the key. Improving management procedures does not help. The procedures help, but they only help in reporting or identifying the productivity process or deficiencies. They do not increase productivity.

I have seen this over and over again. Some executives will reorganize their company and tell the world it was done to increase the company's productivity. Some executives will assign additional reports so they can keep track of the company's poor productivity, only to see the productivity go down because now the employees are busy producing the report rather than the company's products.

The solution to realizing productivity increases is at the level where the actual production is accomplished. There are only two things you can do: improve the environment such that the employee will, on his own, improve the production process, and to recommend your own improvements to the production process. All of this must be tempered with the saying that the improvements must be small. Large improvements will definitely cause failure for your company.

While I do not recommend making large improvements in the process of increasing productivity, I recommend that the institution of small improvements be continuous at the level of the employee actually involved in the production. Improvement must never stop. It must have management commitment and employee involvement—and it must be continuous. Change will not take place without those three features. Your company will not be competitive without them either.

Remember, it must be at the level of the employee who is actually producing the product for the productivity increases to take place. It is the process. It is the environment. It must be continuous.

Incentives increase productivity only to a limit. It takes a proper environment to exceed that limit.

You can only increase productivity so far by giving incentives to your employees such as salaries and bonuses. Most professionals are looking for a challenge in the proper environment at a fair salary. Those who try to increase productivity by offering incentives alone will quickly reach a limit beyond which you just cannot go.

It is the environment that really fosters productivity increases, especially in professionals where the product is the output of one's mind. You cannot produce when you are unhappy. You cannot produce when you feel you will not get the credit for this work. You cannot produce when the working conditions are lousy.

There are many aspects of a proper work environment an executive must manage. The most important aspect is ensuring the worker enjoys his job. If you as an executive spend the majority of your time worrying about the environment, your employees will spend the majority of their time worrying about the productivity.

And what makes an employee enjoy his job? The answer to that is different for each employee, but there are some common traits. Among the most common are job satisfaction, success in accomplishing a task, respect by both superiors and peers, credit when due by both the company and the customer, and the feeling of being a member of a team, not a pawn in a much larger game executives play.

Job satisfaction is most important when you are a professional. You have completed the task and the product works. You don't need anyone to tell you that you have done a good job because as a professional, you know what a good job is. You are pleased both with yourself and your product.

You must have success to continue working at any profession. Success builds confidence. That is why it is so important for supervisors to assign tasks to an employee that is within the ability of the employee. Even assigning a very insecure employee small and simple tasks which he can perform successfully builds the confidence he needs to attempt to perform even more complex tasks. Success is very important in building a good employee.

A happy employee receives respect both from his supervisor and his peers. Without respect, loyalty disappears. Without respect, motivation is gone.

An employee must get credit for the work he performs. As a supervisor, always give credit where credit is due. Don't worry, your supervisor will give you all the credit you need for managing the employee who did so well. When a job is well done, there is always enough credit to go around.

An employee must feel that he is a member of the company team. A supervisor should always use the first person plural pronoun "we." You make that employee feel he was a major contributor to the success of the project, and he will beam with joy along with all the other members of the team.

To be successful, a company must educate its customers. This is necessary to ensure that your customer can ascertain whether someone is merely saying he can do the job or can actually do the job.

It is not true that if you build a better mousetrap, the world will beat a path to your door. In fact, they won't even know you exist. Quality is not a trait people generally consider when buying a product. Most of the time, they consider only the initial price.

Quality is generally cheaper when you take into consideration the life cycle costing, a method of ascertaining the total costs of a product during its life. For example, if you buy a product for $100 and it lasts five years. If it costs you $25 a year to operate the product, then the life cycle cost of the product is $225 ($100 plus 5 times $25). Consider for a moment a different product performing the same thing which costs initially $150 and it also lasts five years. If it costs only $10 a year to operate the product, then the life cycle cost of the second product is $200 ($150 plus 5 times $10), yielding a life cycle cost savings of $25. The average customer considers only the purchase price. For that person, it becomes mandatory to educate them about the advantages of purchasing your product.

In the computer system development business, we claim we can build a computer system that works. Our major problem is that almost anyone in our industry also claims they can build a computer system that works. How can you determine who is telling the truth? If you award the contract to the low bidder, you may not determine the low bidder cannot perform the job until the scheduled completion date, which may be two to three years after the award. By then you are committed to that company and you must finally pay and pay to get the computer system the way you originally wanted it. It might end up costing you much more than if you had awarded the contract to a higher bidder, but one who can develop the computer system right the first time.

What we try in the education process of our customers is to identify discriminators which the customer can use to determine who can really perform the computer system development process. We use discriminators such as: Has the company previously performed successfully on similar contracts? Does the company have a highly developed quality assurance program with a proven track record? And does the management have the commitment to a total quality management approach during the development of your computer system?

You must also educate your customer, reeducate your customer, and when they change personnel, go back and educate them once more. It is a never ending process, but it is the only way to sell in this highly competitive market place.

There are two types of company executives, those who have a job and those who run their Lotus 1-2-3.

After my many years working in industry, I can spot what type of company executive a man is within the first five minutes. There are two types: one who enjoys his job and identifies with the company's product, and one who merely runs his Lotus 1-2-3 and looks at the profit and loss of a corporate entity to determine his actions.

I realize that to be successful, an executive must worry about the profit and loss of a company. But when you only look at the financial statements, you are missing the more important aspects of leading a company and that is your business. You are in business to build a product or provide a service. Therefore, you must worry about that product or that service.

During the 1960s when international conglomerates were in vogue, executives had so many vastly diverse businesses under one umbrella that the only thing they used to determine success was the bottom line. Business schools produced graduates who became masters of looking at their spread sheets. But they failed to look at the product or service.

By the 1980s, we had more and more companies run by "investors" instead of people who were in the business. I am particularly sensitive to the airline business where a few investors with their Lotus 1-2-3 spread sheets ruined perfectly good airlines. Almost all decisions were made relative to the cost of the current level of service.

There was little thinking about how to improve the service to get more customers or retain their current customers—but only cuts made after looking at the Lotus 1-2-3 spread sheet to see if they could make more money.

Don't get me wrong, I'm not against using spread sheets, and I'm not against Lotus 1-2-3. I'm just against those who use Lotus 1-2-3 spread sheets at the expense of running the business. Fortunately, there were other airlines whose executives spent most of their time worrying about their most important source of service, their people. They spent their time supporting their people and their people spent their time providing the best airline service to the public. The profit and loss of the company showed this.

Give me an executive who is excited about his product first and about the maximization of his profits second and I will show you a good company.

Executives who manage solely by quarterly financial statements will have neither the right employees or the right products for the future.

This saying is similar to the previous saying, but with a slightly different inference. Executives who manage solely by looking at their Lotus 1-2-3 spread sheets manage for the short term only. Trying to maximize profits each quarter will not prepare your company for the future.

The gestation period for developing high quality employees is lengthy. They are not just sitting out there waiting for you to hire them. They must be trained, both formally and on the job. It generally takes at least two years for a person experienced in computer programming to be at the level of productivity in our unique niche in the computer industry.

It costs money to develop and to keep good employees. Once developed, it costs money to continue their education. Unless you are willing to spend some of your potential profits on the development and maintenance of your employees, you will not have the right employees for the future. Things are changing too fast not to develop your employees and also spend money developing new products or improving your service. If you have the right employees—by developing and maintaining them—they will, if there is a true corporate commitment, develop new products and improve your service. But there must be that true corporate commitment. Lip service just does not work. Employees are not dumb; they can see through anything other than true corporate commitment any day of the week.

Employees and products need to be nurtured. They don't just grow on their own. Those employees who can grow on their own will quit and form their own company. It is a constant process.

All this nurturing must be tempered with good business sense. If you go overboard with the expenses, you will do both your employees and your product harm when you go bankrupt. There must be a balance. Don't maximize this quarter's profit at the expense of being in business five years from now.

I have been involved with five-year plans of large corporations. These plans contain sales projections for profits and potential customers and contracts. I have never seen in these five year plans where there is a section describing how the employee will be ready for that new business. There may be a section on new products, but not the method in which the new product is to be developed or improved. These financial types merely allocate some money in the proposed budget for internal research and development and that's the end of it.

The five-year plan should concentrate on improving the people, the product and the service.

To prepare for the long haul, 80% of your effort should be spent on improving the work environment and 20% on the product or service.

Now that we are beginning to identify the fact that we should concentrate on the employees and the products or services, we must then determine the division of our time between the two. You cannot do it all. By the very definition of being an executive, you have many people working for you, both directly and indirectly. This is necessary because the volume of your business demands more than what you can do alone. Now that you are in that position where you do not produce the product or service, just what is your job? It is to create the environment where others produce the product or service.

It is my belief that approximately 80% of your effort should be spent on improving the work environment. If you worry about your people, they will worry about developing your product or providing your service. A president of airline cannot fly every airplane; he cannot serve every meal; he cannot sell every ticket or handle every bag or service every aircraft. His job is to improve the work environment for those who do all those tasks. His job is to establish a fair salary structure. His job is to ensure that there is job satisfaction at every level, that there is a chance for all to achieve success, that there is respect for all from all within the company, that there is credit given when credit is due, and that the company is the team.

As an executive, you are the coach. You worry about the team. The team plays the game. You must also, however, worry about the product or the service, but only about 20% of you time.

This is where many executives fail. They feel that they can let those engineers do it. Those engineers, however, while highly capable, sometimes lack the vision of a leader. Sometimes all it takes is to tell an engineer a glimpse of an idea and he can take it from there. As an executive, you must provide the vision for the product or the service.

In many cases, this vision is really a member of your staff's idea. That's all right. Give him the credit. You don't need the credit; you are already the boss. But make the idea a part of the company's future. Your employee cannot do that. Yes, he can come up with the idea, but it takes you to make it officially part of the company. It takes you to provide the vision of where the idea fits.

The free marketplace is the only true distributor of one's products.

I do not believe that there is anyone intelligent enough to develop a system to determine the distribution of a product. The planned economies of Eastern Europe are living proof of this. The only true distributor of a product is the free marketplace.

This is so basic to marketing, yet there are those who are continuously trying to devise a better system. Yes, there are inequities in the free marketplace, but in the same manner as Plato chose democracy as the least of the bad forms of government, we must choose the free marketplace with all of its inequities. Yes, the philosopher king was the best until he became the tyrant. Plato wisely rejected him as a good form of government, yet men are still trying to develop planned economies to replace the free marketplace.

The reason or justification for the free marketplace is just that—it is free. The seller is free to try to sell his product or service, and the buyer is free to buy the product or service. If there is no buyer for the product or service—regardless of how good it is—the seller must begin to sell something else or go out of business. The buyer buys only what the buyer wants. It's free choice.

Now consider what would happen if there were a completely planned economy. Some person determines the products, the quantity of these products, and the price of these products for a particular region. The demand may or may not be there. If the demand is not there, there will be a surplus of the product. If the demand is there and is excessive, there will be a shortage of the product. Since he also determined the price, the price cannot be used to correct a surplus or shortage of the product. This even goes as far as the salary of an employee.

I remember my conversation several years ago with a government employee with a master's degree criticizing our economic system because he as a GS-12, was making only $12,000 a year and he knew an eighth grade dropout who had started a garbage collection company who was making $80,000 a year. He believed there was something wrong with our economic system that would allow this to happen, especially considering he had the master's degree and the other person only had an eighth grade education (almost).

What he didn't understand with all of his higher education was that the demand for garbage collection was greater than the demand for his profession. The free marketplace had established their respective salaries and they were right. If this person was given his own way, salaries would be determined by some means having nothing to do with the law of supply and demand, but with his perception of worth. Once we accepted such a system, it would forever be doomed to the subjective judgments of some bureaucrat.

Bureaucrats, no matter how good their intentions, can not mandate the distribution process successfully.

During the oil shortage of the fall and winter of 1972-73, I was engaged in a conversation with several of my colleagues in Washington, DC. We were discussing a mutual acquaintance who was working for the Department of Energy. One of our colleagues asked rhetorically, "Do you know what she was doing?" We all said no. He said that she was allocating gasoline to certain areas for distribution. We all knew this girl was very intelligent, but not intelligent enough for the job of distributing gasoline in the Washington, DC area. There were lines up to two miles long waiting to obtain gasoline, while only fifty miles away in West Virginia, there were no lines at all.

I know the intentions of both the Department of Energy and the girl were good. The distribution process simply exceeded their mental ability. We were convinced that day that if the U.S. Government would have left the distribution of the short supply of gasoline to the free marketplace, the lines would have been significantly shorter. A service station with a small supply of gasoline and a long line of vehicles waiting for that gasoline would raise his price (basic law of supply and demand). Another service station with a larger supply of gasoline and virtually no line would lower his price. Soon the word would get around and the vehicles in the long line would leave and go to the service station with no lines. Within a day or two, equilibrium would have been restored.

Even at the distribution level, a distributor would see that he could make more money sending his gasoline to the area with the higher prices and suddenly, the shortage there would disappear. As the prices began to fall, the distributor would choose some other area to sell his gasoline. This would continue until there was equilibrium in the distribution process, and so on.

Immediately after any deregulation, management will underestimate the cost of doing business and will underprice their goods and services.

Being in the aviation business, this saying and the one immediately following are the result of observing the airline industry for the last twenty years. We saw some of the most phenomenal changes ever seen in any industry. There were new airlines, mergers of old airlines, and disappearances of airlines almost as fast as there were appearances of new airlines. There were cheap airlines and expensive airlines. It was really mind boggling.

What we were seeing was the adjustment from a fully regulated industry to a completely deregulated industry, and there were many new entries into the airline industry. Each of these entries was led by a management team that knew they had the answers to compete with the older established airlines. However, many underestimated the cost of doing business. Even the no-frills airlines with their super cheap fares underestimated costs.

Why? Didn't they have the experience of running an airline? Well, yes they did, but not a deregulated airline. During the whole period of airline regulation, no one knew just how efficiently an airline could be run. Then there was the competition! You had to lower your price to get the passenger, but you lost money when you lowered your price. The only way to survive in that environment was to have deep—I mean very deep—pockets.

Take a look at the airlines that have survived and are doing well now. Each one of those airlines had deep pockets. During the first decade, almost every airline startup bit the dust. They didn't have deep pockets. They either were purchased by an airline with deep pockets or they went bankrupt. Then there were giants in the industry that went bankrupt.

We thought we had quite a deal with all those cheap fares. We thought we had competition among the airlines with all those new startups. But where are they now?

The actions necessary to correct these underpricings will not take place until the second decade and will then be viewed as overpricing.

Then we began to have airline executives with ten years of experience in the deregulated market. They began to realize the real costs of running an airline in the deregulated market, and they began to adjust their fares such that the airline becomes profitable. (A somewhat radical idea, becoming profitable.) Now the U.S. Government is beginning to discuss regulation again because the fares have gone up. We had these cheap fares for ten years, now it is time to pay the remainder of the fare. We just have to pay the piper.

Bureaucracy is a system of distrust. Because of this, we demand before the fact an act is in complete agreement with our rules or our interpretation of our rules. We demand this regardless of the cost.

Bureaucracy has taken a bad rap for centuries. Bureaucrats have been categorized with tax collectors. But it is not really their fault. Nobody trusts them.

Bureaucrats must execute a system of distrust. This system consists of implementing a set of rules or interpretation of rules that are designed to ensure the system works as the makers of the rules intended.

Most of my experience is with government bureaucracy. I experience this both as a private citizen and as a government contractor. I have discovered that bureaucracy has two major characteristics: It is a system of checks, and it is a system of obtaining prior approval.

First, the system of checks. Someone must check everything you do. Your immediate supervisor must check your next act. Contracts department must check your next act. Legal department must check your next act. And so on, until it takes three months to complete a simple task such as order office supplies.

Second, the system requires prior approval. This is where the distrust really hits you. No one trusts you; therefore, you must get their approval before you do anything. If you have to take a trip, you must get your supervisor to approve the trip and determine whether

the trip is necessary. You must get the travel department to approve the trip to ensure you are going the absolutely cheapest way. You must get the accounting department to ensure the budget has money to pay for the trip.

Where do all these rules that the bureaucrats must execute originate? By tracing the origins of these rules, at least those I experienced in my private life and in government contracting, I have discovered their origin being in our own U.S. Congress. Virtually every rule that bureaucrats must execute results from a law passed by

97

congress or an interpretation of a law passed by congress.

Someone violated the trust that must exist in any relationship. There was a public outcry. Congress acted—or should I say reacted—by passing a law whose sole purpose was to ensure that trust would never be violated again. The poor bureaucrats—and I really feel sorry for them—now have the responsibility to ensure no one will ever break the new law. They first identify all those who have the ability to determine if a planned act would break the law. These usually involve the immediate supervisor, perhaps his supervisor, legal, accounting, contracts, etc. Now this requires you, the poor bureaucrat, to submit a detailed description of your planned action to each of these people so they can ensure you are not breaking the law. As each of these people review your detailed description, they make small modifications. You implement these small modifications and resubmit it. You then submit the modified detailed description to the next one on the list. They make small modifications to it which require you to resubmit the detailed description to all those to whom you have already obtained approval, and so on. It is no wonder that things seldom get done.

Rarely does the original law address the cost of executing this law. It immediately assumes that all bureaucrats are incompetent or are crooks. This is not true. More than 99% of all bureaucrats I have met are competent, honest, and loyal. The system they must execute is incompetent.

I, too, believe that there should be high morals and trust in our relationships with the government, but why punish the 99% of the bureaucrats who are honest and moral and trustworthy?

Bureaucracy cannot accept the concept of spillage. It has to be perfect.

These laws that bog down the bureaucratic process assume perfection. They want a perfect system. They cannot accept the concept of spillage.

For example, the concept of spillage is prevalent in private industry. If a company is producing a widget on an assembly line with a quality assurance check at the end, they are willing to have a less expensive production process and throw away a few widgets at the end. There is a point of diminishing returns. To reduce the number of widgets thrown away, the production process must be improved. It is when the cost of improving the production process exceeds the value of the widgets that are being thrown away that the manufacturer ceases to improve the production process and accepts a certain level of spillage.

The same concept applies in the bureaucratic circles. When the cost of implementing a law exceeds the cost of the wrongdoing, then don't implement the law. If you discover a government employee violating the rules relative to taking business trips, fire him. Don't punish all those honest and trustworthy bureaucrats who would never think of violating the law by requiring them to obtain all those approvals. It costs money—a lot of money—to require all those approvals.

Yes, some will get away with violating the rules for

a period of time. A few will get away with violating the rules for a long period of time. One or two will get away with violating the rules for their entire career. But even with these losses, it doesn't even come close to approximating the costs of executing the normal rules bureaucracy makes to ensure it can never, never happen.

Perfection assumes a human trait that does not exist.

We are not perfect. Perfection is not a human trait that exists. Any rule based on the assumption that perfection exists is always prohibitively expensive. Most of the excessive costs of our government are the direct result of trying to be perfect. We can not do it. So why try? It is far better that we determine that point of diminishing returns and accept the concept and cost of spillage.

Any policy, law or rule is only as effective as the acceptance of the policy, law or rule by those to whom it applies.

People will only obey that which they accept. Do you remember those great days of prohibition where our government tried to abolish the act of drinking alcoholic beverages? The law was never accepted by the people; therefore, it was not obeyed.

At the same time, there was a law against murder. This law was accepted by the people and, therefore, was obeyed by the vast majority of the people. (Let us not forget the 1% of the population who are kooks; they don't accept anything).

This is especially true within a company. Executives are constantly making rules by which they expect employees to abide. Executives must first determine if these rules are acceptable to employees if they expect the rules to be effective. You cannot arbitrarily make rules. Oh, they will probably abide by the rule for a short period of time, but only grudgingly. They will begin to ignore the rule completely. The rule will cause desertions amongst the employees and privately, in conversations in the hallway and restrooms, they will make comments about that stupid rule made by that stupid boss in that stupid corner office.

A policy, law or rule will only be accepted by those to whom it applies if they see a direct benefit from the policy, law or rule.

Before an employee will accept a rule, he must see a benefit. The benefit may be that it helps the company and in turn, it helps the company keep the employee employed. But the employee must see the benefit. All rules without benefits—whether direct or indirect—are considered stupid rules, and stupid rules are never followed very long.

If you cannot find the benefit for the employee in any proposed rule you are thinking of implementing, don't make the rule. Rules in and of themselves are not good rules. Talk to your employees about the situation you are trying to correct with the rule. It may very well be you don't need the rule; all you need to do is to fire that bad employee who committed that act you want to eliminate by the rule. Implementing too many rules in your company institutes a system of bureaucracy you definitely don't need.

Be willing to accept the concept of spillage. I have found it better to trust my employees—not require the paper work a system of distrust demands—and fire any violators of my trust. Treat your employees as professionals and 99.9% of the time they will be professionals. Treat them otherwise and they will become exactly what you expect of them.

The direct benefit from a policy, law or rule may not be immediate. If this is the case, the authors must educate those to whom it applies as to its benefits.

Many times the benefit from a policy, law or rule is not immediately obvious. For example, doing anything now in preparation of something that may not happen for two or three years or even worse, may never happen. I think of the many things we keep in the personnel files of our employees. Most of these things are to help us in that rare case of a disgruntled employee who was fired and is now suing us.

We established the rules for maintaining the files on each employee in anticipation of such an action. We have never had to use our personnel files for that purpose. We would like to think it is because we treat our employees fairly that we never have disgruntled employees.

Nevertheless, you as the executive must educate those to whom the policy, law or rule applies as to its benefit. It is relatively easy to explain the benefits of the law against murder. We all yield to a law against murder and we can live a life relatively free of fear of being murdered.

But let us take the case of social security. You are twenty-one years old and that large chunk of your paycheck is taken under the guise of preparing for your retirement. Hey, I need the money now! How do I know if I will ever receive any retirement? I may not live that long. Here is where it is necessary to educate the people as to the benefits of the social security law.

If you are unable to educate the people about the benefits of your proposed policy, law or rule, they will not accept your proposed policy, law or rule. Then where are you? The burden of proof is on you.

Wait a minute, you say. I'm the boss. Yes, maybe, but you are trying to get your employees to design, develop and install that very complex computer system that is pushing the state-of-the art. That computer system is the output of creative minds, and unhappy minds are not creative. Work with your people. It is the only way. This implies receiving a consensus of acceptance of your actions. Anything else will cause you to lose the very people you wish to keep.

That is where the rub is. Almost everything I have written in this book serves to create an environment to keep your best people. Whenever there is any problem, it is normally the best people to go first. They are more intelligent, generally, and they can see what is happening. Because they are intelligent, they are more marketable and other companies really want them. Do you want another company's bad employees? No. You want their best. The same is true for them.

No matter how effective one's rules, regulations and systems are in assuring a good relationship between two corporate entities, it will be the mutual trust and respect that will yield success.

In so many of our corporate relationships with other companies, it always appears that the people administrating the relationship rely more on the rules, regulations and systems than on mutual trust and respect. It is the trust and mutual respect that oils the machinery of working together, not rules, regulations, or systems.

Rules and regulations are generally based on distrust. This rule was put in place because a company or a person several years ago violated its trust. That regulation was put in place because the company wanted to protect itself from breaking a law. I know they are needed but they are based on distrust, and what kind of relationship is a relationship based on distrust.

Let's take the case of systems. In most cases, these systems were developed to facilitate the reporting of day to day actions such that the customer can monitor the company's actions. Why monitor the company's actions? Simple. The customer does not trust the company. The customer wants to monitor continuously the actions of the company to determine if and when the company is in violation of the rules and regulations.

Mutual trust and respect come from each party entering the relationship expecting the other to perform their part and themselves to perform their own part.

Mutual trust and respect are required before any relationship will work. This is true regardless of whether the relationship is personal or corporate. It seems that in personal relationships you see mutual trust and respect more often. But in business, we must be cold and callous, which is another way of saying we don't trust or respect you.

Corporations are made up of people, people just like us. They put their pants on one leg at a time just like we do. They have wives, they have children, and they have all the joys and problems of having wives and children. If they are people, why can't we trust and respect them?

We must therefore expect them to perform their job. At the same time they must expect us to perform our job. There is just no other way.

Rules, regulations and systems relative to a relationship between two companies establish minimum standards only. Minimum standards do not promote success.

When you rely entirely upon rules, regulations and systems to maintain a corporate relationship, you will not have success. The reason is obvious: Rules, regulations and systems establish minimum standards only. You must rise above that.

For example, let's assume you are in a meeting with the other company and you both discover a major problem that must be solved immediately. The other company is the prime and you are the subcontractor. The solution is out of the scope of your contract with the prime. Therefore, a contractual modification will have to be made before you can legally begin to solve the problem. You agree on the statement of work. Then, the presence of trust or the lack of trust enters on the scene.

If there is trust between the two companies, you will begin to solve the problem as soon as you get back to your office, knowing full well the other person will begin to process the contractual modification as soon as he gets back to his office. Even if it takes one to two months for the contractual modification to be finalized, there is the trust between the two companies that both will perform as promised at the first meeting.

If there is no trust between the two companies, you

will wait for the other company to process the contractual modification, which still may take up to one to two months regardless of the urgency of solving the problem. This distrust will delay the implementation of the solution at least one to two months.

The greatest degree of distrust and lack of respect seems to lie in the contracts department of both companies. There seems to be no concern for the project. There seems to be no concern for the added costs that delays always cause. We will do it by the book, don't ask any more questions!

All of this distrust and lack of respect costs money. I know there are some who just cannot be trusted and respected, but most people want to be trusted and respected. Those who cannot be trusted and respected are in the minority, a very small minority. We try to correct for those in that minority by developing excessive rules, regulations and systems with the idea of never letting whatever it was the rules, regulations and systems were written to avoid happen again.

But why place the costs of trying to correct a very small problem on everyone. Why not promote trust and respect? It is much faster—and with a simple periodic and spot auditing process, it would be less expensive.

When one demands competition in contracting, the buyer must pay for all proposal efforts including the losing ones.

Competition is not a panacea for all perceived problems of the free marketplace. In many cases, there are significant hidden costs in the competitive process. This is especially true in the U.S. Government competitive procurement process.

Let me give you a case study. Let us assume a government agency wishes to buy a major computer system. Let us also assume there are five companies qualified to design and develop that major computer system. Let us assume each of these companies makes a profit and all of their business is with the government.

When a company does business with the U.S. Government, his costs are divided into various categories. These are direct labor costs, travel, other direct costs, overhead costs, general and administration costs and fee. (We do not call fee profit until we have successfully completed the contract and we have money left over after paying all expenses. Fee is just an estimate of what the profit can be.) Included in the general and administration costs are two items called marketing and bid and proposal (B&P). These two items combined are the budget the company has to market its products and services and to prepare and submit the proposals to the government in response to a request for proposals.

The amount in these budgets are based on an estimated gross revenue and are approved by the government prior to an award of a contract. When a contract is awarded to a company, the company receives moneys that are placed in the pool for such expenditures. The company then collects the marketing and B&P moneys from all of its contracts and prepares and executes its marketing plan.

After all of this discourse, the most important thing to remember is that the marketing and B&P budgets pay for all marketing and proposal efforts regardless of whether the effort is successful or not. Since our assumption is that all of our companies were successful—in other words, they win approximately 25% to 35% of all proposals they submit—the government pays for all of the proposals including the unsuccessful proposals, approximately 65% to 75% of the effort.

Think of it. Our government pays for all of the unsuccessful proposals. So when you compute the actual cost of a system, you must include the costs of all the unsuccessful marketing and B&P efforts of the companies who lost. Competition has its costs.

I think the worse cases are when the government has many false starts. They say they want to procure a system this year. You staff up your marketing force preparing for the request for proposal to come out, only to find out they have delayed the procurement by six months. You have already spent some of your marketing money and for what? Six months later you gear up for the procurement, spend more money only to find out they have delayed the procurement for another six months. You are still profitable somehow and these false starts are being reimbursed as part of your general and administration budgets from your other contracts with the government. It does not have to be with the government. This also happens in commercial arena. In the final analysis, it is you, the private consumer or tax payer who foots the bill.

Don't get me wrong, I'm not in favor of a planned economy. I'm just saying there is a cost to a badly managed competitive process. While I do not recommend any changes to a free enterprise system, I do recommend that those who are in the procurement process recognize that false starts, excessive delays, and demanding excessive competition inflates the costs of not only the product you are purchasing, but also all the related products whose price must be great enough to pay for those false starts.

We want the best to be our athletes, doctors, lawyers, etc. and are willing to let them reap the benefits accordingly. Why are we not willing to let our political leaders reap the benefits accordingly when we want them to be the best?

As Americans, we get exactly what we deserve from our elected officials. We refuse to create an environment that lures the best to run for elected office. If you consider that when you combine both the Senate and House, each member represents approximately 486,000 citizens. He is to make laws that govern the most powerful economic force in the world. Yet we place such restrictions on him that the best, for the most part, decide not to take part in the process.

Any why should he? The pay is appalling. Anyone worth his salt to represent approximately 486,000 American citizens should be paid much more. If he was in private industry and was a CEO of a company consisting of 486,000 employees, he would be paid four to ten times as much. Few men who have reached the status we would require would want to take the reduction in salary. Only those whose independent income is so great the difference doesn't mean much are willing to take the job.

Consider the invasion of privacy! Not only your own privacy but that of your wife, your children, your parents, your siblings and anyone else the press and opponents can find. There are few men who have a successful record of achievement that do not have at least one or two skeletons in their closet.

We want the best, but the only thing we offer them is power. We all know that power corrupts and absolute power corrupts absolutely. It is no wonder we are having the scandals in the congress we are having.

Most of these men are honest when they are first elected. Oh, they may have big egos, but that is a prerequisite for the job. I truly don't hold that against them. But here is a man making just over $100,000 a year, maintaining two homes with one in his home state and one in Washington, DC, hobnobbing with lobbyists who are making four or five times as much, tasting power at a level he never before realized existed.

What do we want the man to be? Dedicated? To make a sacrifice, at least financially? I have never trusted a man who does something strictly out of dedication. I have always suspected an ulterior motive when someone says they are doing something just because they are dedicated. If it isn't for the direct salary, it must be for the power and the money he can make on the side. The only way for this not to be true is to elect a man who is independently wealthy.

We allow others who are the best to reap the benefits from their profession. So why not our political leaders?

There is no such thing as a good set of functional specifications from the customer.

One of the first things I learned after I entered into the work place is that there is no such thing as a good set of specifications from the customer. There are many reasons for this.

First and foremost, there are almost always two organizations involved in any procurement: the procuring organization and the user organization. The procuring organization specializes in the procurement of complex systems, but has never fought a war. The user organization has fought a war, but has never specified a complex system. They talk two different languages. One speaks "systemese"; the other speaks "operationalese." These languages are significantly different. Neither organization believes in cross-training; however, both occasionally lace the other's camp with their own members.

Cultural literacy is also different in both camps. Not only do they use different words, they use words that have different meanings and etymologies.

The user community does not understand the system development process or the current state-of-the-art systems in their field. Not having this cultural literacy, they are unable to articulate their requirements. Their only experience with systems has been with the current system and its predecessors that the new system is to replace. They are not aware of the level of detail of the advances that have been made to adjacent fields. They lack the cultural literacy necessary to visualize significant steps forward in the specification of the new system. It is as if someone wanted a new international telephone system and didn't know communication satellites existed.

On the other hand, the system specifiers from the procuring organization have never fought a war. They do not have the feeling necessary in designing a system. Lacking the user experience, they are unable to appreciate what the user is saying. While at the same time, lacking the system specification experience, the user is unable to appreciate the questions being asked of him.

The only solution, from a contractor's point of view, is to create his own breed of hybrids: those who are part system designer and part system user. It requires a great deal of cross-training with gestation periods up to two to five years before a person is able to perform at the desired level. Once in place, they can interpret the specifications received from the customer, identify the deficiencies, and recommend changes to the specifications to the customer before it becomes too expensive to correct.

We have even in some of our proposals recommended that the first task under the contract is to rewrite the system specification and if the rewrite requires a contractual modification, modify the contract. This approach may appear to be arrogant on our part—trying to tell the customer he doesn't know what he is specifying. Sometimes it is, but you must do it if you expect the system to really meet the true mission requirements.

The net result of not modifying the specification at this point is that after the system has been developed, passed the system acceptance tests, and the procuring organization has accepted the system from the contractor, the using organization rejects the system because it doesn't meet the operational requirements. This happens all too often. The customer is then caught in a serious dilemma. He is usually caught with a system for which he has already spent a great deal of money and can only afford the bare minimum to modify it to meet the user organization's mission requirements. The user organization is under pressure to accept the system lacking a great deal of the capability he always wanted but was unable to articulate to the system specifiers of the procuring organization. And we wonder why systems cost so much.

One solution to this problem from the customer's standpoint is to not write functional specifications, but operational specifications. Full functional specifications are very difficult to write. You have to anticipate everything possible. You have to specify to the nth degree every possible detail. If you are wrong, you can be assured the contractor will charge you for the correction. Generally, they will charge you dearly for the correction.

Operational specifications require the contractor to translate the operational specifications to the functional specifications. If you specify an operation for a surveillance system that has the capability to identify aircraft flying at both very low speeds and very high speeds with all speeds in between with a specified accuracy, that is all you have to say. Let the contractor determine if he wishes to use a conventional radar, and over-the-horizon radar, a satellite or 10,000 employees using binoculars scattered over the coverage area.

Really, you don't care how the contractor does it. If his system design meets operational specifications, it meets the operational specifications. Then you don't have to worry about the axiom that there is no such thing as a good set of functional specifications from the customer.

Chapter 4

RELATING
TO
BUSINESS

People actually think corporations pay taxes.

Oops, next book.